A

is for Anna Alligator, who is amusing her animal friends.
Circle the picture words that begin with A.

apple

arrow

acorn

airplane

asparagus

ant

1

B is for bustle at the baseball game.
Circle the picture words that begin with B.

butterfly

bird

baseball

banana

balloon

bat

brush

bee

boat

book

button

bell

C

is for carts of cool food.
Circle the picture words that begin with C.

cookie

cat

cow

cake

carrot

cabbage

D is for Doctor DoGood, the dentist.
Circle the picture words that begin with D.

duck

daisy

drum

doll

dog

diamond

5

E

E is for everyone eating at the diner.
Circle the picture words that begin with E.

elephant

eggplant

earring

eagle

egg

elf

F is for fun at the football game.
Circle the picture words that begin with F.

footprint

flag

fish

flowers

football

firecrackers

G is for a garden of growing plants.
Circle the picture words that begin with G.

gift

goldfish

gold

gopher

goose

gate

ghost

gorilla

grapes

grapefruit

goat

H is for happy hours here on the farm.
Circle the picture words that begin with H.

hammer

hot dog

heart

hippo

hay

hamburger

10

I is for the ice cream inside of the truck.
Circle the picture words that begin with I.

insects

igloo

invitation

ink

ivy

ice cream

J is for joy at the toy store.
Circle the picture words that begin with J.

jam

jaguar

jack-in-the-box

jump rope

jet

jacks

12

K is for King Karl, ready for dinner.
Circle the picture words that begin with K.

koala

kiss

ketchup

kite

kitten

key

L

L is for laughs at the lively party.
Circle the picture words that begin with L.

lipstick

letter

lemon

ladder

leaf

ladybug

14

lobster

lamp

lion

lollipop

lizard

lamb

M is for Mary Moose, having fun at the carnival.
Circle the picture words that begin with M.

mitten

mushroom

music

marbles

money

mouse

FACE 5¢ PAINTING

milk

monkey

moon

mop

mailbox

mask

N is for the nurse who is nice when we need her.
Circle the picture words that begin with N.

nail

net

nuts

nine

needle

nest

is for Olivia Ostrich, talking on and on.
Circle the picture words that begin with O.

octopus

onion

orange

owl

olive

ornament

P

is for plenty to see at the zoo.
Circle the picture words that begin with P.

pipe

paint

parrot

peanut

pen

pencil

peas

pie

popcorn

pineapple

pumpkin

pear

Q is for the queen riding quietly in the woods.
Circle the picture words that begin with Q.

quince

quilt

quarter

question
mark

queen

quail

22

R

is for a rhino on her roller skates.
Circle the picture words that begin with R.

rake

roller skate

rocket

rope

rose

rug

S is for sunning in the sand during hot summer days.
Circle the picture words that begin with S.

snake

sandwich

sock

seal

sunglasses

six

starfish

soup

seven 7

spoon

sun

sailboat

T

T is for two bears on their camping trip.
Circle the picture words that begin with T.

telephone

tulip

tomato

top

tent

turtle

U is for unusual things under the Big Top.
Circle the picture words that begin with U.

umbrella

umpire

unicorn

unicycle

ukulele

V

V is for Violet and Victor, having a very good time.
Circle the picture words that begin with V.

violin
vase
vest
violets
vegetables
valentine

W is for the wonderful wedding of Wally and Wanda.
Circle the picture words that begin with W.

watermelon

whale

worm

woodpecker

watch

wood

X is for Xavier Hippo and **Y** is for his young friends.
Circle the picture words that begin with X or Y.

xylophone

x-ray

yacht

yolk

yo-yo

yak

yarn

yam

Z is for zany stories read with zest before bed.
Circle the picture words that begin with Z.

zucchini

zero 0

zipper

zebra

Camping Out

Circle the hidden pictures.

Find: | 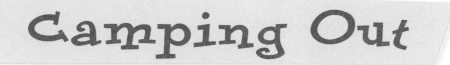 | | | | |

Farm Jamboree

Circle the hidden pictures.

Find: |  | | | | |

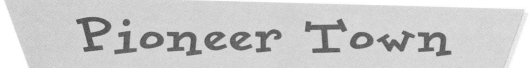

Pioneer Town

Circle the hidden pictures.

Find: | YIELD | R X R | 🏠 | H | ← ONE WAY | 2 STOP

Barnyard Party

Circle the hidden pictures.

Find: 1  1 1 1 3

Into the Sky

Circle the hidden pictures.

Find: 1 [golf clubs] 2 [suitcase] 1 [tennis racket] 1 [umbrella] 1 [newspaper] 3 [EXIT]

At the Zoo

Circle the hidden pictures.

Find: 2 ⊘   2 🐿   I 🦒   I 🍦   I 🧳   I 🍿

The Toy Store

Circle the hidden pictures.

Find:

Where to Go?

Circle the hidden pictures.

Find: 1

A Boy's Room

Circle the hidden pictures.

Find: 2 🧦   2 🪥   1 🧸   1 🎧   1 📕   1 🕐

Grocery Shopping

Circle the hidden pictures.

Find: 2

Dinner for Two

Circle the hidden pictures.

Find: 1 🗡 1 🛡 2 🔑 2 🚩 2 🏆 1 👑

A Peaceful Park

Circle the hidden pictures.

Find: 1   1   3   2   1   1

44

© School Zone Publishing Company

Works of Art

Circle the hidden pictures.

Find: 3 ✏️ 1 🖊️ 2 🖌️ 1 🖼️ 3 🎨 1 🎨

Fun at the Beach

Circle the hidden pictures.

Find: 3 👓 2 👡 1 🧴 1 📷 1 🪣 3 ⛵

Turtle Crossing

Circle the hidden pictures.

Find: 3 · 1 · 1 · 1 · 2 · 2

Pets on the Loose

Circle the hidden pictures.

Find: 1   1   2   2   1   1

3 🔵 1 🔼 3 🕊 1 🦎 1 🏰 2 🦴

Asleep in the Deep

Circle the hidden pictures.

Find: 1 🌊 3 ⬭ 2 🐚 1 🐚 1 🪱 1 ⭐

Elves at Work

Circle the hidden pictures.

Find: 1 🛒 1 🥄 1 🌀 2 💧 3 🐸 1 🔨

Final Frontier

Circle the hidden pictures.

Find: 1 🚀 1 🎈 2 🐟 3 ✏ 2 ✂ 2 🖍

Work Zone

Circle the hidden pictures.

Find: 1   2   3   1   1   3

Anybody Home?

Circle the hidden pictures.

Find: 2      1   3   1   2   1

Dining Out

Circle the hidden pictures.

Find: 1 🐦   1 🏠   2 🪹   1 ⛲   1 🎏   3 🐦

Summer Picnic

Circle the hidden pictures.

Find: 1 🪒 1 🧴 2 🪁 3 📷 1 📻 2 🌿

In the Treetops

Circle the hidden pictures.

Find: 1 2 3 1 2 1

Garden Friends

Circle the hidden pictures.

Find: 2 🐸 3 🦋 1 🌱 3 🐌 1 ☁ 2 ⭐

Clown School

Circle the hidden pictures.

Find: 2 ⬡ 3 🅵 1 ✏ 2 📏 1 🌿 4 ❀

Baking at Home

Circle the hidden pictures.

Find: 1  3 1 3 2

Birthday Party

Circle the hidden pictures.

Find: 4 ⬦ 1 🎂 2 🎉 1 👟 1 🧦 2 📯

Dinosaur Swamp

Circle the hidden pictures.

Find: 2 🦋   3 🪰   1 🐢   1 🦢   1 🐊   1 🦩

Afternoon Tea

Circle the hidden pictures.

Find: 2 🌷 | 🦔 4 🐝 2 ☕ | 🧤 | 🐦

The Busy City

Circle the hidden pictures.

Find: 3  2 1 1 4 2

 Hidden Pictures, Ages 5–Up **02348**